A Gathering of the Leaves

A Gathering of the Leaves

Poems by

Anastasia Chauny & Graham Isaak

Contents

Contents

Introduction

Over the past five years we have been forging a friendship through the written word. Poetry has seen us through many seasons. As these leaves have gathered, the growing piles have marked the passage of time.

For this collection we uncovered fifty-two poems, one for each week of the year. Some of these leaves are freshly fallen, others brown with age, and several dug up from under months of snow.

Anastasia Chauny

Graham Isaak

August

Dog days of August
Plod on until September's
Manic caffeine rush

CONSTANCE

The only changeless thing is change,
  each season has its act.
"Behold, I do a new thing now!"
  is the Eternal pact.
Some nations become multitudes,
  while some return to dust;
Some lions become lambs,
  but all submit to moth and rust.
All heads to equilibrium,
  but lurches on its way,
And only One has wings to guard
  the dusk, the dawn, the day.

OH, WHAT A HEADACHE WAKING IS!

Oh, what a headache waking is!

How pleasantly the covers fold
And wrap you in their warm embrace,
As pleasant scenes of times untold
Do dance across your closed-lid face.

Oh, what a headache waking is!
Though shaking, quaking, making art
Or raking in the time and place
Require waking as their start.

And even though we know so well
How bad we fear to never wake
Still, how we cling to blanket's shell
As if we lie for Hades' sake.

Oh, geez. And now I've made the act
Of simply getting out of bed
Akin to the dramatic facts
Which guard the living from the dead.

Who knew that someone's simple morning
Carried such dramatic storming?
What the Buddhists teach, I'll take:
Existence is a small headache.

PROPRIOCEPTION

How many thousands have lain, back to the ground,
Felt themselves suspended by gravity to the globe,
And imagined themselves rocketing through space —
Flying over a chasm of stars?

Oh Earth, I am inevitably held to your chest
By virtue of that mysterious force which grants
Power proportional to your sheer vastness:
And I am grateful to be so small.

For who knows what horrible destinies
Would have befallen me, unbound and ungrounded?
And though I could struggle and escape,
I have found freedom in being tied to you.

When I rise, how do I know what is "down"
Despite seven billion other opinions?
Only your gravity is the synthesis of our perspectives:
Space-time morphed by your molten heart.

And I am grateful to be so small.

RESTING STATE

Beneath the sun
In tree-shadow
There sat a boy.
He didn't yet know what he hated.
He could imagine a better sun,
Another tree,
A beautiful companion;
He could imagine a quieter street below,
A richer job,
A more comfortable city.
And he looked around in the little space around him,
And he couldn't imagine getting to know its every
detail,
Its grass and weeds,
Its shadows and patches of light,
The slope of the ground,
The wash of the breeze,
The dust of the lungs.

September

Dog days of August
Plod on until September's
Manic caffeine rush

FRIDAY NIGHT AT THE HOUSE

Tick, Tick, go so many cogs and wheels.
The old Grandfather sways his pendulum
With a senility that borders on drunkenness.

Hickory-dickory-dock is the old rhyme,
Though the mouse is long gone
And no one stares
At the cryptic analog face —
Behind it, so many wheels are turning.

Seconds tick through day and night while
He sits in the same dusty shadow.
Yellow lights leak from the living kitchen.

Rock, Rock, go so many circuits and wires.
The red Radio blasts his speakers
With a cacophony that borders on mind-numbing.

"Social Drinking" is the accepted euphemism,
Though the partiers are too far gone
And no one listens
To the low fuzzy lyrics —
The result of so many wires pulsing.

Music floats through air and bodies while
He sits on the same grimy counter.
Brown-blackness creeps from the vapid hall.

Clock laughs at Radio, wasting energy
On background noise for everyone.

Radio laughs at Clock, as he stands alone
Forgotten, ringing for no one.

Neither moves.

SONNET – "JUDGMENT-FREE"

I wish I was a free-of-judgment zone,
Where people could find love no matter what.
But "judgment-free" is free for me alone;
The person's still imprisoned in their rut.
"Judge not, lest ye be judged" - so reads the Book,
Comparing how your measure measures you;
With logs across your eyes, how can you look
To safely tweeze the speck from brother's view?
So, tweezing brothers find themselves condemned
By sharing lack of clarity in sight;
But meanwhile, those who see the truth can mend,
While those who don't, won't, try hard as they might.
    What outdoes "judgment-free," and frees to live?
    Forgiv'n by one who knows what they forgive.

ELIXIR

The leaves fall like green-tinted snow

Trapped in gauze, a verdant glow.

Steam breathes into all my pores

Liquid flame to calm the sores.

It's what you always turn to

When the hard times get to you

You said to me

Just drink the tea.

The miracle, the cure-all; healer

Antioxidant magic dissolved in water.

But I wonder if this bitter cup

Can heal you with your mouth sewed up.

Your words were few

If only, if only I knew!

But all you said to me

Was drink the tea.

I can't drown my worries

With a few shredded leaves.

A universal medicine

Should be able to invoke conversation.

The cup of life has no substitutes

I need pure water to nourish these roots.

But here I am, see…

And at my lips is tea.

PAINT NITE POEM

For Y.

You paint my life
In the corners,
In places
I never had thought to see colour before.
Your paint in my life
Leaves its traces
In borders;
New orders appear, and I notice them more.
You're simply astounding my old sense of colour,
Abounding in sights I had not before seen;
For now, in my life
There's a new kind of paintbrush;
That faint touch of you
Is the paint
That I mean.

October

October dark falls early
Leaves fall, candles grow brighter

A LIFE WITH MORE BROWNS

Some paint a life out of rainbows and gold,
With colours and roads of good cheer.
But I want a life with more browns and more cold;
A life where I've really *met* fear.

I swear that they gave me a good education,
And told me one day I would fly -
But I'd like a life with my feet on the ground;
And I'm not sure if I can spell why.

ORANGE DAWN

An ode to the Southwestern United States.
Inspired by a flute piece of the same name by Ian
Clarke.

Breathe the sky
Feel sandstone grit
Red Mesa stands tall
Hear soul-flute echoes:
Kokopelli in the canyon cliffs.
Breathe the blue sky
Twice as big as any other sky
Turquoise and silver paint
Spread on this firmament and
Placed over orange rocks.
This is a sanctuary
Land of arroyos and bison
The air is thin enough
For the spirit to fly
This solitude of land and sky—
Breathe it!
Tranquil silence, a last vestige
The only corner on Earth
With these lizard-warmed rocks.

THE SLIME MONSTER

In my house there lives a creature
       that I rarely ever see
And in fact, I've never seen it,
       but I know that it must be
For whenever I'm away from home
       for any length of time
I come home to find the kitchen
       polka-dotted with green slime.

How the monster operates is
       something of a mystery
And I'm sure if I could watch
       it'd be phenomenal to see
How it tries, but fails in its attempts
       to keep itself contained
Since the floor is often speckled
       with the food of its remains.

How I feel for those chickpeas,
       and that garlic, and that paste,
Getting first so poorly treated,
       and then rashly thrown to waste!

But I feel bad for the monster too,
      whose vision must be crude
And whose hands must be so clumsy
      that he fails to grip his food.

If he showed himself in daylight,
      I don't know what I would do.
Would he suffer harsh rebuke?
      Or would he spatter me with goo?
Would he give up vegan-ness
      and promptly eat me, saying "See ya!"?
Well perhaps I'll ask my roommate –
      maybe he'll have some idea.

TO A FORGOTTEN MEMORY

There is something I know I'm missing,
A word that isn't on the tip of my tongue,
A blade of grass that died some summers past,
A puzzle-piece hiding
In the lightless cavity of my mind.

I try to picture what it should look like
But I'm starting with less than an empty easel,
No backdrop or foreground,
No white noise, no, no sound at all,
And it smells like gibberish,
Without movement or stillness,
The air empty of temperature.

On some month-day-at-time
I shaped it, or maybe it shaped me
And for some amount of hours,
Worth their weight in gold,
I smiled, or I cried, or I pondered.
I lived. But, like gold, it was heavy.
The words I thought or perhaps exchanged
Rolled around and dropped out, unnoticed
Like an anchor lost to the depths,
Its rope severed somewhere in the waves.

I would search, but for what?
It's as useless as
Framing strangers' photographs.
What truths did I learn in that moment?
What inspirations and images did I see?
I hunger for the fleeting thoughts.
Oh memory, what would you remind me?
If you ever had the chance?

HE LIVED IN A WORLD THAT DIDN'T EXIST

He lived in a world
That didn't exist,
Though he claimed it was no less true;
And year after year
He would plainly insist
That it might make appearance to you.

For he looked at the things
That were underneath things;
The things that were hidden from view –
And he looked at the fringes,
And weakening hinges,
And there he found plenty to do.

There were trolls that were stern;
There were dragons who'd burn
In a strangely familiar way.
And the pigs couldn't fly,
But they could say, "My, my!
How I envy the pigeon today!"

There were elves who were spirits
In charge of all secrets,
Delivering near ones and far;

There were wolves who would howl,
Too trapped in a scowl,
Too frightened to slow down and starve.

There were brightly lit places,
Where, leaving no traces,
A special event could take place;
You'd return in the morning
And know, with forlorning,
You'd never return to that space.

In his world there were owls
Who asked other questions,
And love songs that sometimes sang hate;
There were hermits with wisdom,
And heroes in prison,
And leaders weren't always irate.

What a world, he thought,
Is this world I live in;
How strange, and how noble, and blue!
I won't bother myself
If it doesn't exist;
For I find it not any less true.

November

Baked goods herald friends
November, December joys
Filled with Advent pause

BUYER'S REMORSE

Nondescript but exotic,
Nutritious and nutty,
Cashews on my plate—
Don't they look funny!
Rough, curled, and tan,
Expensive but bland.
What dish should I make
To sate my demand?

Should I simmer them long
In a curry or stew,
Or should I just roast them
A minute or two?
Should I garnish a salad?
Make cookies to bake?
They just look so naked—
Can't swallow them straight.

Somebody picked out
All these cashews with care.
Someone sold them at market,
Their flavor to share.

But why did I buy them
(Some marketing ploy?)
From the natural-foods store,
Who robbed me with joy?

I'll just crack one slowly
Into its two parts;
I'll chew them to bits,
These small, buttery warts.
As I sit in remorse
And I wrack my poor brain—
I just wish I'd bought almonds
And saved all this pain!

FOR A GREAT MAN

For K.

Laughing with Ku is a great thing to do.
It's as if you're omitting a sentence or two.
It gives intermissions to halting admissions;
It speaks a permission; it listens to you.

When you're laughing with Ku,
You're sharing what's true.

Laughing with Ku is a good kind of laughter.
It's deeper, and stronger, and rings on long after.
It's a laughter of one who has struggled and vexed
With the questions of Why?
And of What's to come next?
And emerged, not unscathed,
But less mad and perplexed.

When you're laughing with Ku,
Your laughter takes tunnels
You both have gone through.

When you're laughing with Ku,
Then you've met a new dawn;
For it's rare that one meets
Such a man who *hangs on*.
And it's this, of all possible hid qualities

That goes often ignored; that can cause great unease
But is rather essential if people want peace.

When you're laughing with Ku,
You're releasing what's hidden;
It flows from the dark
As if comfortably bidden.

We can practice both sides,
And trip up on the question:
In life's great swing dance, are we leader or follow?
It's best to consider another suggestion:
What matters is whether our laughter is hollow.

When you're laughing with Ku,
Then your laughter gains richness.
The thing you held on to –
You're ready to ditch this.
You'll face what is forward.
You know this is true
When you're laughing with Ku.

WHITE HEALER

Come, white healer, as season turns,
Lay your hands over these raging burns.
For a time, for a time.

Muffle the harsh traffic sound
And cover up this littered ground.
For a time, for a time.

Ice the wounds of prejudice,
Erase our politics with grace,
For a time, for a time.

Drive our homeless into hearths
Make us battle cold, not hearts,
For a time, for a time.

Protect the earth from trampling feet,
Cease industry's productive beat,
For a time, for a time.

Hold us, crush us, teach us peace
Till springtime thaws bring new release.

SWELL AND FADE

Swell and fade, swell and fade.
What season is this?
Bell and blade, smell and spade -
Winter mint on counter laid,
Mem'ry stirred - swell and fade,
Fade away, you winter hint of summers gone.
Some are gone;
Others come along in season.
Reasons, none; just as well…
Fade and swell, fade and swell.

December

Baked goods herald friends
November, December joys
Filled with Advent pause

ACCORDION-SONG

For K.

Play him a new accordion-song,
My friends! An accordion-song,
As his spirit departs and his soul swiftly wends
To the future for which we all long.
If your hope is that Christ will re-make us a life
Where dear Nana will get a new hug,
Then come play the old man an accordion-song –
As he runs to the riches of Love!

WINTER NIGHT IN MONTRÉAL

We don bulky space suits
Stuffing pants into boots
In white plastic insulation
We march out in trepidation
With fur at the hood.

Will warmth and ease
Be sucked from these small bodies
To the ever-frigid stars?

Facing infinity, suited people
Passing by each church steeple
Like satellite-docking stations
While snowy comet-dust constellations
Squeak beneath our feet.

As our moonscape swings away
From sun and light of day
We are on the cold face.

SEED POEM

For A.

A long, long way away and many Christmasi ago,
A farmer sowed some seed along a field all in a row.
That seed grew wheat; was made to bread;
Was shipped, and sold; and bought, and fed
Into a young man, newlywed,
Who one night took his wife to bed.

The woman later did give birth
To a smart chap who roamed the earth
And decades later, chanced to stop
Inside a tiny coffee shop.

How curious, how strangely fair
Were all the words imparted there!
The seedlings sown; their force unknown –
And did they fall on earth, or stone?

The farmer sits among his cedars
(The same whose seed had fed the breeders)
And never knew the seed he'd sow
Would feed a man whose seed would flow
When in the mood, into his wife
And seed the birth of someone's life.

Now (pardoning the man's erection)
When it comes to "Will of God,"
I must reject His firm direction;
Often its results are flawed.
Yet contemplating farmers' seeds,
And coffees shared, I can't deny
Delighting in the so-uncanny
Routes which good things travel by.
(And, hipster sus-chord builds aside,
It seems that there's no place for pride
When contemplating holy hands
And things that no one understands.)

BEAUTY

She might have wondered
Mary, that is,
Why the son of heaven would have been born
With such an unsightly mole.
Or maybe sometimes his disciples
Had a hard time getting people to follow a prophet
With a lazy eye.
He, that great servant
Might not have even been picked for a slave
On account of his bad teeth.
The God of perfection took up ugliness,
Put on weight in the wrong places
Maybe even walked on water with a lopsided gait
Ankles turned out
Would you listen to him if the paintings
Depicted such a man?
What dose of beauty do you deem necessary to
Swallow a philosophy?

STARBOARD SEARCHLIGHT

There was nothing but ropes and wood
      to keep me company
The black of night, cloud covered stars,
      the gently tilting sea.

The creaking planks, they spoke to me
      through watches of the night,
I thought I heard the cry of gulls
      that circle land in flight.

But no, no sight of rock or bird
      would come to me out here.
My dreaming mind's invented shapes
      were all that I found clear.

I held my lamp high as I could;
      its scattered light was cold.
It went not far, and lit no more
      than waves, like garment's fold.

The train of the Eternal's robe
      is what I sailed upon;
It cloaked straight paths in mystery
      and covered up the dawn.

And rocking, twisting, tossing there,
      I thought my candle vain
Unless it could, with feeble glare,
      my hope somehow retain.

But Lo! Another flame sprang forth,
      far off the Starboard bow—
Someone like me, I had not known,
      was sailing there, somehow!

O happy hour! My night-time watch
      has brought me great reward,
My lamp held proud, I sing aloud
      my soul with joy outpoured.

And though we might be ignorant
      of why we sail, and where,
We are at least two, floating near
      with lighted lamps to share.

January

Starlight spills on promises
In the New Year afterglow

HONESTLY

Some days the carpets fall, and then
I pray a bit more honest prayer
It's full of "shits" and "fucks" and stuff
And other things residing there
In that walled cavern that must be
The fortress of my honesty.
(In case you visit: it's the stall
that has a mask hung on the wall.)

STRONG AS DEATH (SONG OF SONGS 8:6)

Call it nature's noble rule,
Or treasure from devotion's trove,
But fleeing it will kill the soul.

Intimate, umbilical,
An archetype, the Lamb, the Dove
Call it nature's noble rule

The End exerts its lovely pull
And passion fits it like a glove
And fleeing it will kill the soul

For her, a woman at a well
The pouring-out would prove his Love.
Call it nature's noble rule –

It's candle against waterfall
The kind unyielding as the grave
And fleeing it will kill the soul

So am I wise, or just a fool?
To love the Scorned, who gave it all
And call it nature's noble rule
For fleeing it will kill the soul

FUNERAL COMPLEX

Here in the House of Death, many crosses overlook.
There is a desperation in our cries.
>   *Please. Please. Let this be the answer.*

Here we've built a safe haven to lives that have ended.
Can we not build such things for lives that are being
lived?
>   *Please. Please. Let there be an answer.*

Our neediness
Curiously murmurs
Under the mumbling of the secretary.
Potted plant and electrical heater,
Calmness of reflection,
Hum of lighting,
Certainty of death,
The mystery of its meaning.
An end?
A resting place?
Peace at last?
Somewhere better?

Here the stones cry out in worship.
Perfect squares of marble, unbreakable walls
Laced with the traces of the past
Which crawl their way through the glimmering
surface,
Crying out for escape,
To break through,
To not let the impenetrable gleam have the final say.
   Please! Please! We know, there will *be an*
answer!

The living are lucky to hear the stones,
To walk among the mystery of the dead
And be thankful that its call is far off,
Or near at hand
But not yet set upon us.
To feel a heartbeat pulsing where one ought not to
Is to have faith,
To understand creation speaking promises
Whose word will be kept
Beyond the time our beat fails.

I come here to see what my deeds will arrive at,
To remind myself of the futility of my lofty planning,
Of the flagrancy of my selfish desires;
To reset the lens on my distorted self-image.
To meet and to be met.
And yet

To be here is never an ending,
For on the day we are brought here without our
choosing
We have already ceased to be.
Every visit to the unknowable future
Is an invitation to the present,
To live with our feet on the ground,
To know connection, and love, and heartbreak,
And defeat, and solitude, and challenge
And discovery and bearing witness and
Seeing and knowing
And not knowing
And eventually

Hope.

PERSECUTED OPTIMISTS

It's slowly, slowly creeping in.
That old refrain that "life's not fair"
Grows more in truth and sense each day.
We children in our sheltered world
Live under siege, and oftentimes
A missile penetrates our walls:
Fathers dead, friends paralyzed—
All you can do is wait and pray
And hope one day the world will make
A bit more sense than it does now.

The real world out there jeers and yells,
And some within start to give up.
A woman's babe does not see light,
The laid-off workers disappear,
The smiles are drowning in a sea
Poseidon, where confusion reigns
And Aphrodite never laughs.
All you can do is wait and pray
And hope one day that we'll be more
Than persecuted optimists.

February

February slumps
We forget promises and
Curse our luckless love

INACTION

By steering ill, my soul is often tainted;
And with selfish ambition, well acquainted.
But equally I'm tempted by distraction,
And know too well the evil of inaction.
"Perhaps it's best to take a rest."
"No, no, my son! Keep moving on!"

STAINED GLASS

It's cold inside
And the color is gone.

The songs are sung
To all and no one.

For the doors are shut
And the music is stuck,
Echoing on deaf ears

Where grace is not luck
Rather it is earned.

So the vibrant hues
Seep out stained-glass windows
Leaving white pews.

It's cold inside
And the color has left

Because all the smiles
Of false warmth are bereft
Of joy and of reason
Of rhythm and rhyme,

And this place feels like treason
(robbed of its last line).

Therefore take me outside
Where the color has gone;

Let me run in your sunlight
And sing that old song.

OF APPLES AND TRUE LOVE

The way it used to be
The apple didn't fall far from the tree.
Now they pluck it while it's green,
Gas it with sweet ethylene
Wax it like the glossy floor
And put it in your grocery store.
Its sisters all stand side by side
And customers grab, smiling wide
The very same flesh Eve first bit
And think no more of it.

I'm guilty too; I've felt its blood
Running down juicy and cold
On my chin and then I remember
It's winter, past December.
How synthetic is my existence
That I'm only in the present tense?
No room for seasonal rhythms within me
Persuaded that now is all that will ever be
The aroma is overpowering,
They tell me that's a natural thing.

My will is no longer my own.
I think they've put my soul on loan,
Thinking they can mass produce
The taste of home-grown produce
With airbrushes in magazines
And glorified erotic movie scenes
Laying open skinless slices
Worshipping all human vices
And cutting out the core
So love has no meaning anymore.

But the way I think it used to be,
Blemishes weren't so unsightly;
Hunger was only one of our needs
And we'd always re-plant the seeds.

FATHER, SHOW US THE WAY TO ROMANCE

A quick road to shame is the path of "the mood"
Which we let be our bane and our fall,
Forgetting the game: title "One Becomes Twoed" –
And with what desperate longing we call.
God's family's full of "successes" and "failures"
And folks who just beg for a chance
Yet we colour it crude; the pursuit, the pursued.
Father, show us the way to Romance!

We hide what is ardent; we ask it be pardoned.
Our Passion we think is a snare.
But – hold on. You're saying Your power's made perfect
Exactly right then and right there?
Forgive us our sins! Lord, forgive us our weakness!
Adultery hides in each glance;
Yet is there a place where you wash clean our face?
Can we ask for any more chance?

O Lord. You're confusing! We want to be *choosing*.
We want to know who's in control,
But – (God, is she *neat!!*) – when we're swept off our feet,
Lord, we don't want to fall in a hole.

We're people of pride. And we think we're enlightened
In how we can live *our* designs.
We want to take flight. And to think: You delight in
These children you called into mind!

Let us watch with delight as the sepia changes
And years of together make known
All the corners and colours of knowing an*other*
Whose heart and whose mind is Your own.
How helpless we'll stay, till Your sons and your
daughters
Rely on Your heart for our plans.
Now, bring your son home, where his bride waits
alone.
Father, show us the way to another dance day,
In the rhythm of Heaven's romance!

March

By March the delirium
Of weighty work peaks—distract me!

ID

There's fire down there
That burns cold
Roots grow down
Centuries old
Creatures—
Forms, twisted and bold
And all stories
As yet untold

The only place
You'll never be
The side of the mirror
You'll never see
What you still
Choose to call "me"
Moves below
Unconsciously

So draw it out
Bait it, and lure it
Throw your dice
And make a gambit

This dangerous mistress,
Who hates your wit
Is the instinct that
Never does forfeit

And though it does
Thrash about blindly
You wrestle, deciding
That you'll answer kindly
Use its own weight against it
Heap the coals on, divinely
Your heart will be broken
But just mildly.

Under the earth
Under your tongue
It feels like darkness
But it's under the sun.

CONSCIENCE

You ought to know how talented my conscience thinks
I am.
It thinks I am a genius;
(It hates when I admit to this)
It think I am a genius;
Just what my precious genie is
Is "TBA,"
And so, one day,
I'll find out with a **WHAM**,
And all will give a damn.

You ought to know how terrible my conscience thinks
I am.
It thinks I am a dictator,
Misogynist, and dick-hater
Whose talents as a leader
Are as weak as Mary's Lamb.
And when I start to dwell on this
(Which I do all too well; honest!)
It twists the gears between my ears
And gets me in a jam.

…My conscience is a scam!

How could a good Creator be
So full of jealous love for me,
A thing so contradictory?
And yet, I find in those I love
Their contradictions rest, and stay,
And shift, and change,
And twist, and stretch,
And still they seem to operate
Effectively enough.
So when it comes to loving me,
Perhaps it's not the end of love
If things so contradictory
Pop up, stick out their neck, and stuff.

THE ART OF TRYING

She tries to reach and catch the sky
But stumbles over rocks and roots,
The details keeping her from dreams.

She thinks she knows what it all means
And yet she lacks the words to speak,
Sufficing with a desperate cry.

Her fingers hold back music's flow
As she sets them on the keys or strings,
Ten reasons she should just give up.

She pushes on, but wants to stop
Ever-elusive expression's pursuit.

FOR WEAK SAINTS

"You shall love intensely," says the Lord.
"You shall better understand the storms and mountains
Than the fields and the lakes,
Except where these lakes are deep, and their far shores
unseen.
You shall undergo arduous journeys and never get to
see the view.
And though you seek Me, I will run from you,
So that you seek Me further;
I will flee, so that you will not give up the chase.
You will rest, but only for a time.
Like a sailor, you will see a beautiful sunset as a
threat,
Drinking the beauty of its red light so as to heed not
your dread of the morning.
You will be given to much wandering and restlessness,
And thus shall you know loneliness;
Yet also shall you know the restorative company of a
person,
The mysterious stranger met on the road;
The heroic, quiet Character who truly lives.
You shall believe relentlessly in magic and childhood
And also in journeys into darkness,
Knowing that those born in light must see the night so
that they know what the light is.

And you shall see freedom only where others see
hopeless oppression,
And you shall see cages where others see comfort;
And you shall be blamed for your lack of eyesight.
With God's tools one may chisel away at your heart,
In His Fire will it melt;
In the unusual detail of His creation will it start to
beat.
Empty of its old inhabitants,
Unnamed city, fallen into ruin;
A ghost town devoid of meaning.
And I will populate you!" says the Lord.
"And I will rename this city, and give it its broken
king with a heart of flesh!
Dying and reborn, baptized and rebaptized,
Fallen and lifted, over and over,
Thirsting for water, surprised by wine,
Sword that was broken,
Clothing refashioned,
Armour of righteousness,
Hamstrings burning in reluctant obedience,
Faithfully hoping,
Come back
Again."

April

Lucky, the earth turns
April alternates hope and
Chilling, rainy days

SHADOWS OF THE TREES

One writes of life devoid of ease,
Of stronger wind, and tougher trees;
But in this age, where brains beat brawn,
Our hope in trees of strength is gone.

But trees are more than strength of wood.
Our breath is what makes greenness good.

Winter shades the fall's revision;
Urgent pleas to false religion
Cut across the seas beneath
The air of each forbidden leaf.

Sky of orange, yellow, pink,
Fade to purple, greyed to link
City lights against the moon.
Pity night must fall so soon!

The softling air; its riffling touch;
The lightning bug which loves so much,
And in the air, one whistling hue;
The ope'ning of an avenue –

And in the clouds, and through the breeze,
And in the shadows of the trees,
The secrets lie, for us to find
Beyond the reaches of the mind.

FIDDLE DUM AND FIDDLE DEE

Fiddle dum and fiddle dee
Nonsense words to melody,
Fiddle dee and fiddle dum
Dance to mental lute and drum.
Fiddle dey and fiddle doo
Let me sing a song for you,
Fiddle doo and fiddle day
As we make our merry way.
Feedle die and feedle dim
Joy is founded 'pon a whim,
Feedle dim and feedle die
We'll play our hearts out by and by.
Feedle deedle beadle doe
What we're saying goes and goes,
Feedle foedle simple ding
Mumble stumble dawdle sing.

FOUR LINES

Depending on finding a close- or near-rhyme,
A wild set of words you must tame,
You'll find that you practice, like music and math, this
Four-cornered and innocent game.

The first is a line that says any odd thing,
The second foreshadows the last;
The third is restricted, but more so convicted;
The fourth brings resolve to the past.

But how do you show how the rhythm should go?
So many have tried this, and failed.
How can you intuit the way you should do it
So that your work isn't derailed?

The feel of the words, and the bounce of the beat
Is what makes the reading a breeze;
If you can recall where the emphases fall,
You'll see language is all twos and threes.

Don't look for a function in every conjunction,
A meaning in each little verse;
We've got to be ready for what is ahead.
Performers all have to rehearse!

'Twas Ernest said "Shit" describes every first draft;
So don't criticize your work in fear.
Just let your shit flow; later, edit below
Till expression becomes more clear.

And everyone knows, though you put it in prose,
No matter how toughly you try,
The power of poem to drive a point home
Is something we cannot deny.

MY HERO

My hero was a fat man.
He liked to sleep
Flat on his back,
Hands folded
With his belly poking up in the air.

And when it was time
For presents
Or dessert,
He told us we could wake him;
And wake him we did.
Right next to his ear,
We'd yell,
At the top of our lungs:
GRANDPA!

MULTIVERSE

I floated in space
        making dreams in my head,
Each dream was a world, its laws to obey
Whatever I said.

There were dreams that made sense,
        consistent and true.
They were user-friendly, and harmonious
To listen to.

Complex yet straightforward
        summations of laws,
All life that lived there, without any falt'ring
Echoed my calls.

And then I decided
        they were void and empty,
These rational worlds, without beauty or pain
Were worthless to see.

So I dreamt one last dream
        that consumed my whole mind
With conflicting laws, and dissonant chords
In space and in time.

Intrigued and in love
        with my feet on firm ground,
For once in my life I'd found worth and a cause
Brilliant colors and sound.

So forever I've chosen
        this earth's crazy laws,
Pulled myself through its loopholes and walked
Right into death's jaws.

May

By May it's a crescendo
One more hurdle to summer
Balconies feel feet

GIVING IT UP

Once a year on Good Friday
We all, disciples, walk away
And leave behind that sorry sod
Who'd seemed to be the Son of God.
And this year, it's with some relief
I go without a shred of grief -
(Though some might find this statement odd)
- relaxed that it's not *me* the God.
No miracles have left these hands;
No saving grace came from my plans.

Had I been at that sorry hill,
I would have stood there, sorry still,
Denied him to this scary crowd,
Then stood in silence, judging, proud;
And, saving ev'ry grief of heart
To put into my private art
I'd write it down, to think *I* might
Turn all those hearts to sorry flight!

No matter; for when three days came
Like doubting Tom, I'd do the same
And say, "This must just be a rumour,"
Till I'd gone and felt each tumor.

Then, upon my knees, I'd shout,
"Here's what salvation's all about!"
and try to claim it for my own.
"Here, brothers, watch! I'm saved!" I'd moan.

So, what relief to know: the Lord,
Without an army or a sword
Did come to save humanity,
Including selfish men like me
Who doom ourselves to dumb frustration
Meant to measure our salvation.

Lord, forgive this lusty heart
Its thirst to play the righteous part,
And let these lips instead confess
That Christ has authored righteousness.

THE RICH MEN IN DEATH

(Isaiah 53:9, Easter Dawn, and Summit Circle, Westmount, QC)

We walked between tomb
After tomb in the cold:
The rich men in death—
Or perhaps just in sleep.

When hope had grown old
We walked to the tomb
Too tired to weep
Too drained to be bold—
The rich men in death.

Yet climbing slope steep
With myrrh for his folds
We walked to the tomb
Of Him without deceit
Who was buried, behold,
With the rich men in death.

And whom did we meet
In that sunrise so gold?
He walked from the tomb
The man, rich in death.

PARIS

City of wanting
City of women meant to be desired.
Here no two streets align;
No two souls meet.
This is the city of romance,
The city of not having,
The city of pursuit,
Of mystery,
Of elegance waiting to be revealed,
Like the liberty of which they dreamed.
Yes, this is the city of romance; but not of love.
It's the city of envy,
Of beautiful women who don't speak,
Of monuments to this, that, and the other;
A place to stay,
To fight for,
To have passion in,
But not to live.
This is Paris.

STONE PRINCESS

For my Father, who sees millenia in every rock.

She kneels on earth, eyes to the sky
A living, abstract statuette
She stands and doesn't move, and I
With feet upon her roots, feel small.

I wonder what life seems to her
Whose eye sees ages pass in blinks
Cool and calm to human blur
While magma licks her granite toes

The rivers, angry, carve their beds
Into her lovely, weathered flesh
Embedding her with liquid threads
While clouds spit rain upon her face

The wind howls secrets to her ears
And when she cannot stand one more
She sheds boulders like tender tears
Crashing down from trembling cliffs

Yet she is strong, to make birds sing
To catch the stars in glassy pools
To cloak herself in green each spring
Though crumbling, like us all, to dust.

June

They plan for June and beyond
Those two weeks off with the kids

GUILTY SURFACE

An insect flew into my eye.
One blink, and it was over.
You never know when death is going to strike.
Blinded by what I could not see,
I fisted my eye red
Trying to wipe clean the
Guilty surface.

MOTH

Wings dusty from disuse
I slept in the day—
Or maybe my nature
Has made them that way.

The smiles of dreamers
Are of little use;
Nightmares, for that matter
Seem also obtuse
If the hopes and the fears
Are forgotten with waking,
I'd rather be conscious
Awake and remembering.

Here in the night
I fly and I sing
Fluttering back and forth
Ceaselessly searching;
Even if it kills me
The flame I will find
For I'd rather see
Than be happy and blind.

Of what worth is courage
Not knowing what you face?
Why take up a cross
If you don't know its weight?
I'm drawn to the fire
Though I know it burns
Its warmth and its light
Are too much for words.

They call it folly—
Those greater than I
But instead of live sheltered
I'd knowingly die.
That's my intent,
But as we all know
On getting too close,
I'll flee from light's glow.

Who is to condemn
The fact that I try?
So at twilight's close
I take wing and fly.

BEE IN THE WINDOW

Frenzied, frenetic
Pushing at the glass
I watch her, wings a-buzzing
She doesn't know
This transparent technology
Straining toward the sun
Without a backwards thought
Longs for light
But cannot reverse-engineer
Her inauspicious arrival.

She is dangerous, but
I want to end her desperation.
I hesitate, her heaving abdomen
Speaks despair, resignation
Wings folded
Will she hibernate
Perpetually between panes
Till death takes her?

Will flowers unfurl, furl,
Untasted, wasted
This bright sunny day?
Will she never fully feel

The honey-balm heat
She lives for? I approach,
Strain at the latch—
Fearful, I can already feel
Her sting—

Window creaks wide
Unattached, fly, be free!
I step back swiftly.
No movement. Too late?
Regretfully, I return to work.
Fighting back thoughts of failure
Until, at day's end, I look back
To find her gone.

ONE MAN

For S.

One man shouldered a heavy load,
Thinking himself on a lonely road.
He fought in vain to set himself free,
Till a man came along and handed him a key.
And they said:
>   Still your journey's as confusing as before.
And he said:
>   Well, sure. But I can open up a door.
And more and more of the pieces found their place,
Till he looked back over years to see the arcs that they
had traced.
And if life has storms, and rainbows are the promise at
the end,
Then one needn't look for pots of gold
When one has got a friend.

July

Barbecue smell wafts
Lazy, idling is the norm
July is too short

STETHOSCOPE (NIGHT DRIVE)

The words spill forth, garbled garbage
Your trash, this girl's treasure.
Do you examine your pearls?
Waste, diamonds, waste, gold
The Universe has a pulse.

I know of what you speak.

Young to capable and back again
In less than an hour's journey
You are so timid yet confident
Child, adult, child, grown
The Universe has a pulse.

Paradoxes.

Poets' conversation, under shy stars
Something keeps us alive for now
Beneath this intimate heaven
Stay, leave, stay, go
The Universe has a pulse.

And the world, it changes around
So set your feet on solid ground
I know of what you speak
But are afraid to believe.

Do you examine your pearls?

And the world, it crumbles to dust
With paradoxes that feel unjust
I know of what you speak
But are afraid to believe.

They only seem like contradictions
Gold waste, grown child, go stay...
Dark light, dead life...
All part of the punctured flow, vital.

The Universe has a pulse.

And the world, it has a heartbeat;
I dare you to search for it.

LUNAR PULL

We're moving as the moontug pulls;
We're reaching through the brine,
To grasp a hand no longer cold
But broken, by design.
Look up! And face the remade flesh,
His great cosmetic art –
How humbling to be swept along
In longing for his heart!
Again, again we come your way,
Romanced into your fold,
And greet, with new surprise, the feet
And hands no longer cold.
A body which will bed no more
The prison of the grave –
The moon bids hope. To Christ the shore –
We are a tidal wave!

A DIFFERENT KIND OF AMBITION

Hot summer nights
Would find him staring up at stars
With enamored friends
Picking out patterns and naming them.
Shining solitary points
Of silver on black, like faint voices
In a sea of silence...
Those faraway and scattered fires
Stared down unforgiving
Their dances made him dizzy
He wondered how
They could ever burn in such cold
Without oxygen
Without hands to hold.
So his mind would wander
And he would feel the warm grass
Tickle his neck
And smell the vapors from
The afternoon rain
And guide the ladybugs from his finger
Onto twigs and leaves.
He synchronized his breath
With heat waves from the massive earth
And held the ground
For dear life—

As the days passed on one by one,
Some friends made machines
Learned how to launch themselves off
Of this little marble
And into the land of swirling stars.
But he was one of the ones
Who stayed to live under the trees:
A different kind of ambition.

FUTURES

Staring at futures…
The next great adventure…
Afraid.

Shooting at sunsets.
But how do you join the
Parade?

Anger unbidden;
A sofa to sit in;
A reason to ease in,
To soar up, or store up –

A boulder to push, yes, a big heavy boulder,
A lifelong strong meaning-filled burden to shoulder –

Yes, everyone's searching,
But what are they finding?
A load.

Everyone's moving,
But where are they going –
Uproad?

SMILE WRINKLES

I want my wrinkles, in old age, to smile.
I hope they speak for me some decades hence
When wheelchairs and dementia lift the veil
Of hard-bought comprehension, competence…

Yes, life will weather every growing thing
But we must choose which winds we turn to face,
Which buffeting we take upon our cliffs,
And which gorge-carving rivers leave their trace.
In searching for the sea, we must decide
On one of two sides at the Great Divide.

Great love and thoughtless sacrifice are built
Upon foundations of integrity.
We dig into our Id, its soil and silt;
We anchor on what's left amidst the scree
Until the bullet-threats sway not from truth
Or saying till the end, "I love my God."

And that split-second instinct to protect
A stranger from that red-light-running car
Is nonetheless a learned, constructed act
Through deciding to love men as they are.

It's sidesteps over mop-trails, guilt confessed
It's thoughtful gifts and self-examination,
Those prayers for warzones, flowers smelled and
watched,
Prisons visited and money given,
Those extra hours at work, those diapers changed
And running joyfully through heavy rain.

These pave the way for souls to weather storms,
So even cancer cannot steal their forms.

End

And hot. August here
Again to sap energy
We re-start the cycle.

ACADEMIC CALENDAR

Form loosely based on a Renga

Dog days of August
Plod on until September's
Manic caffeine rush

October dark falls early
Leaves fall, candles grow brighter

Baked goods herald friends
November, December joys
Filled with Advent pause

Starlight spills on promises
In the New Year afterglow

February slumps
We forget promises and
Curse our luckless love

By March the delirium
Of weighty work peaks—distract me!

Lucky, the earth turns
April alternates hope and
Chilling, rainy days

By May it's a crescendo
One more hurdle to summer
Balconies feel feet

They plan for June and beyond
Those two weeks off with the kids

Barbecue smell wafts
Lazy, idling is the norm
July is too short

And hot. August here
Again to sap energy
We re-start the cycle.

The Authors

Anastasia Chauny is a fantasy, sci-fi, and poetry writer. Hailing from Denver, Colorado, she moved to Montreal to pursue her PhD in neuroscience. When she's not writing or watching geeky Youtube videos, Anastasia can be caught playing Dungeons and Dragons with her husband Lucam or practicing her flute.

Graham Isaak is a fantasy, poetry, and musical theatre writer and composer. Raised in Winnipeg, Manitoba, Graham came to Montreal to study music performance and French. When he's not writing, Graham can be found running up and down Mount Royal.

www.ingramcontent.com/pod-product-compliance
Lightning Source LLC
Chambersburg PA
CBHW021329060726
47591CB00006B/1933